Volume 115 of the Yale Series of Younger Poets

What Noise Against the Cane

ȝ&

Desiree C. Bailey

Foreword by Carl Phillips

Yale

UNIVERSITY PRESS

New Haven and London

PUBLISHED WITH ASSISTANCE FROM
A GRANT TO HONOR JAMES MERRILL.

Yale University Press books may be purchased in quantity for
educational, business, or promotional use. For information, please e-mail sales.
press@yale.edu (U.S. office) or sales@yaleup.co.uk (U.K. office).

Set in Yale and Louize typefaces by Dustin Kilgore
Printed in the United States of America.

ISBN 978-0-300-25654-3 (hardcover : alk. paper)
ISBN 978-0-300-25653-6 (paperback : alk. paper)
Library of Congress Control Number: 2020943899
A catalogue record for this book is available from the British Library.

This paper meets the requirements of ANSI/NISO Z39.48-1992
(Permanence of Paper).

10 9 8 7 6 5 4 3 2 1

Contents

Foreword

"I am I" — the opening words of Desiree C. Bailey's *What Noise Against the Cane* are an insistence on being, an assertion of self. They also — not coincidentally, I believe — are the words with which Robert Hayden concludes his poem "The Tattooed Man," a poem that addresses the conundrum of identity, of reconciling the self we know ourselves to be, the self we consciously present to the world, and the self that others see through the lenses of their own assumptions and biases, fears and desires. Bailey's speaker here, in the book's opening long poem "Chant for the Waters and Dirt and Blade," is an enslaved young woman in the French colony of Saint Domingue in 1791, at "the onset of what will be known as the Haitian Revolution," Bailey tells us in the poem's epigraph. "Chant for the Waters and Dirt and Blade," like the book itself, has the epic sweep of another Hayden poem, "Middle Passage," but Bailey's choice to present slavery and revolution via the sensibility of a single young woman brings an added intimacy that reminds us that history is always also personal, as is the violence that punctuates history, at someone's expense. Sometimes this means the victims of violence:

> our bodies shoved into the mouths of discovery
> civilization's march towards more
> and more   comforts
> for the cult of the whitened god

and sometimes those who inflict the violence:

> in this garden the white man veils his face
> from his gods   shears the land for it to look like him
>
> in the leaves' tender shadow   he poisons the soil
> with his spilling anger   his barbed sorrow

I spoke of epic sweep. In the course of Bailey's poem, the speaker has her physical journey, but it's the psychological journey that strikes me as the main quest here. A quest for freedom, yes ("freedom never forgets where it once roamed . . . stalks me" and "freedom: ruthless siren"), but also a quest across and through the ever-restless sea of memory. Bailey's speaker tussles with the idea of memory, wanting but failing to remember herself, her origins, at times:

      I   somebody   I   daughter
of seagrass I don't always remember

and sometimes regretting memory:

I want memory to fail   I want
to drive it out with the scent of pésil
to crush its mocking skull
pound it like garlic in a pilon

and at yet other times not wanting to *be* remembered, especially if the form that remembrance takes is offspring condemned to the same suffering that the parent suffered:

I won't leave
no memento of me
if the great god grants me
one thing

no sons or daughters
to stock the mills
no sons or daughters
pockmarked with price

This metaphysical restlessness brings to mind St. John of the Cross's *Dark Night of the Soul;* there's a similar movement toward what is and isn't knowable — here, the self, rather than any divinity — and a similar need to move past, break free of, the earthly experiences that obstruct true understanding. Which is to say, there's something inherently spiritual, as well, to Bailey's poem. Spiritual and metaphysical and epic? Why not? "I am no hero," Bailey's speaker says, but eventually — perhaps via the divine intervention of the sea itself, that has always been there, singing in italics across the bottom of each page of this book (about which, more later) — the speaker knows this much:

when my sea-spirit enters
I am cast from my body's tethers
I am no slave
I am the first language
spinning spinning
beyond the fields

and the result is a new spirit of resistance:

> I begin again   I begin
> in black smoke washing
> the island   barreling across fields
> into the sea
>   what of country   of nation
> of child's palm in my palm then
> leaping through small streams
>   what do I know
> but my body now   my body making
> itself free   onward onward
> toward a beginning   in one hand
> my machete   in the other the sea horn
> the conch blaring the notes of my song

"Chant for the Waters and Dirt and Blade" makes up the first section of this two-sectioned book. After a poem grounded in the eighteenth century, what follows—the rest of the book—is a grouping of poems whose speakers may as well be Bailey herself (who after all gives voice to a poem's speaker if not that sensibility through which any given poet both sees and imagines the world?). By this arrangement, Bailey invites us to see what twenty-first-century life is like for a young woman of the Black diaspora in the long wake of a history of slavery, brutality, and struggling for freedoms bodily and psychological. By implication, the young speaker of the opening poem is the historical analogue for the contemporary speaker, serving as a kind of ghost and guide and tutelary god all at the same time, as Bailey's poems enact a more contemporary quest. Here seems a good place to remember that "quest" and "question" are etymologically related, both originating in the Latin for "to seek"—to find may be the implied goal, but it isn't the guaranteed one or even, perhaps, the most honest one:

> I want to say I am from nowhere and everywhere. But that feels coy like I am lifting my skirt
> for the empire's gaze. Even if it is true. On my papers and certificates, there is a country and
> another country. I can reach beyond, trace the soils through a strand of hair or swab of cheek.
> But what after? Forever lineage riven and ruptured. So I search only because I can . . .
>
>   ("Guesswork")

Yes, a longing for a time "when pain was predictable and understood, when it had a clear cause: the prick of a needle, the lick of a flame" ("Malady"), but longing won't make it so. The searching may be — may have to be — the point, Bailey suggests, the quest enacted via questions that, instead of settling for easy answers, understand the answerlessness as part of what it means, mostly, to be human, but especially to be a particular human whose lineage is the brutal history so (disturbingly) beautifully laid out in Bailey's opening poem.

That poem took place in Haiti. But Bailey, born in Trinidad and Tobago, and raised in Queens, New York, knows well what it means to come from a country torn by colonialism and slavery, and indeed to live in a different country built from the start upon — and by — slavery. It means

> The new school wants to know if I can read *cat, dog, hat*. I think they think big words don't exist on islands.
>
> ("First American Years")

also

> On a field trip to a museum, a white boy I don't know tells me he's glad Martin Luther King, Jr. is dead.
>
> ("First American Years")

And it means growing up with the dailiness of police brutality toward Black people and a concomitant vacillating between mitigated joy when the victim survives:

> Abner Louima survives the police. The horrors of his assault on loop. Three major surgeries to mend his body.

and the ongoing lament for those who don't survive:

> Amadou, O Amadou. Like all Black innocence: chopped down, stolen,
> gone too soon.

It also means, as if inevitably, assimilation as one attempts to belong, only to realize the disturbing cost of assimilation:

> You are clutching a book
> blotting the ink with your sweaty palms
> shoving the words into your mouth
> practicing, repeating, drilling an American accent

sloughing the saltwater off your tongue
speaking yourself into disappearance.

("Extra Virgin Olive Oil")

This risk of disappearance can get tangled in (mistaken for?) a desire for, if not erasure exactly, then an alternative, a revision, or as Bailey puts it in "Woman in Dub":

a B-side where I'm abolished from emotional labor aka black woman's burden free to surrender to my own madness   to sink down into the dub of it   stripped of my first voice reverbing outside the pain of a body —

The dub of the poem's title refers to the reggae tradition of removing lyrics (most, if not all) from an existing song—comparable to the poetic tradition of erasure. The speaker in "Woman in Dub" (which is divided into Side A and Side B) gets her longed-for B-side, a quasi-erasure of the poem's A-side. And sure, the ending of the second section feels triumphant:

free in sound

I   a fact
                answer of my own making

But what—pointedly—hasn't been erased from the original is the ongoing context:

down in the dub   cop hounds my blood
into paranoia   a black reality

Ultimately, though, Bailey reminds us that joy has always been a good counterweight to, if not a remedy for, despair. In her notes on her poem "Orfeu Negro/Black Orpheus," Bailey is critical of the movie for its "simplistic, idyllic, and patronizing depiction of Afro-Brazilians," but the poem itself opens by showcasing (celebrating?) the kaleidoscope of Blackness (colors, emotions, psychologies), goes on to ask "Aren't we charmed and exquisite, dancing as we've always danced," and culminates in what looks to me like resilience:

Where a black falls, another

dances up from the soil. Happy blacks, cycle
of blacks, kicking up dust.

If there's a model for resilience, in may well be the sea that not only informs the psyche of anyone raised near it (I speak from personal experience), but is the timeless repository and reminder of human history, the sea that remains always present even when one isn't conscious of it. Bailey reinforces this idea by having the italicized voice of the sea run along the bottom of each page of her book. This sea speaks with an island accent ("my best approximation of the spoken colloquial form of Trinidadian English, which the late poet Kamau Brathwaite would have called 'nation language,'" Bailey says in her notes to the poem), and tells her (yes, the sea here is female, didn't you know?) own narrative, like the chorus in Greek tragedy—but unlike the chorus, the sea here is never passive. Instead, Bailey gives us a sea that's bawdy, philosophical, and knows full well that she is the center of everything, despite what the poet herself thinks:

> *I was at di center ah dis book, ah what she call it? Di narrative. But she, Miss Poet push me out!*
> *Okay, lemme talk truth.*

And the truth, says the sea, is that our poet only *thinks* she understands herself vis-à-vis the sea:

> *She say she di captain, di boss woman, di one with di pen. She say she cyah be here fuh how many*
> *years wrestlin, gettin fling up in di waves. She say somethinbout di human bein at di center, yuh*
> *know, di one she dream up from history.*

What the sea understands—and therefore can teach, maybe even be the catalyst for—is transformation. Human suffering may be a large part of the sea's song:

> *All ah dat, all ah dat hurt and grief and hope and rage. All dat stolen life,*
> *dat raw weepin deep into me. Dat is di notes ah muh song.*

But by the book's end, the sea sings of insistence, of resilience:

> *All I know is I stayin right here, spinnin wind and spittin, flingin rock,*
> *shell and seaweed against di coast, spreadin high and wide, survivin how I survive.*

This resilience feels both analogous to—and a catalyst for—the transformation with which Bailey's final poem here, "Chant for the Waters and Dirt and Blade (Slight Return)," concludes:

I belong to the foam that singes
the sand where I was thrown to the waves
just weeks into the world my eyes widening
to limestone cliffs to sea almonds ripening
upon the shore my hands are the scarlet ibises
soaring the salt-washed dawn
cleaving the sky open like a blade

Is this the sea's magic? Or the magic that's possible once we remember what we too often forget to listen to – the original self, the sea in ourselves? Like the best poets, Desiree C. Bailey – quite correctly – doesn't answer these questions, but invites us to carry them, to remember to keep asking them. And to remember that to know the self might mean moving past what we think we are, who we've been made to think we are; only then might we find something beyond ourselves that may turn out to be, incongruously (in the way that mysticism is incongruous), closer to what we've always been:

I'd like to stitch myself to the divine. To stitch myself, there must be no me. I must cover the me to make room. I must dig and bury the me. Which is to say I am floating on the light.
("Flowers Pressed to My Head")

Carl Phillips

What Noise Against the Cane

＆

"So much had fallen into the sea. Hats fell into the sea. Hearts fell into the sea. So much had fallen into the sea."

— Edwidge Danticat, *Claire of the Sea Light*

Chant for the Waters
and Dirt and Blade

The brutal French colony of Saint Domingue in the Caribbean.
1791. Onset of what will be known as the Haitian Revolution.
A young woman, enslaved, yearns for freedom,
guided by the goddess of the sea.

I am I   but I won't spill my name
not here on this damned rock   pushed out bloody
from the bowels of the sea   marketplace island
where the cloud's crest and birdsong all for sale

profit of my black   my stewed puss on the plate
in the belly of my captor
                         what am I   what dare I
greased up to quiet the squeak   a howl camouflaged
destined to burst forth   murderous as a wave
meek today   tomorrow cupped for my inheritance
of rage   my name soldiers up like bile   but I dare
not allow it   swallow it bury it
down with the other human parts   of me
I husk of girl orphaned   at the ocean's distant edge
before ship   before humid choke of hull
before trade winds splintering me off into the world's directions

a girl   an I unbroken and spotless   smooth as obsidian's kiss

Crow does fly high but when he come down ants does eat out he eye. And di breeze keep on blowin like

5

the hull   the scarred dark   grave of transformation
where my skin began to crack and molt
girl I was   left behind   in the sheddings
blown overboard   hauled along the endless current

in the current she got wind of me
   she   crowned in cowrie   goddess
of saltwater   glistening   from matted hair
to tail I a shriveling I when she got wind of me
 sinking into sweat   scorch of piss
our bodies' waters overcoming me

out on the deck I measured the ocean
 how it could crush me in its depths
 I rolled death along my wilting lips   slipped
my tongue   into its sweet marrow   how I called
to it like it was my mother   my spine yearning
to be sucked clean

she   creature   mercy
of scales   refused this offering of my body

claimed my head but wouldn't swallow me

she never even know crow name. And di ants love meat when it sweeten by a great fall. Hear how di

she hurled the eye of her voice at the ship
spinning a dark-throated refrain   into the traders' ears
calling them toward the sea

songs of salt   of breasts   nipples gleaming black
like pearls   a lone sweet peace   in sargasso weeds

those ghost-toned men   ached to pierce an opening
to fling her meat   across the horizon
thrusting a cave for their greed

they moaned   pulsing for a lick of her brine
tearing at their hairs   clawing their sunburned faces

but from the hull   another tune waxed
   stuffing their ears with the memory of fortune
      drowning the fish woman's song:

treasure we   sacred cargo we   bruised
pus-filled with promise   of their blood-gold and godhood

ruin make music in di bones. I hear how she drum on di remains before washin it into muh wide wet

oiled up and thrown
down   in the dirt   in the gasp
between the pine-cloaked mountains

I haunted by the land's beauty
its dark face ringing with the throat of a bell

the beauty a curse that trails me at night
stands my hair up like men
in the croon of the mapou tree

O hurt-song
   of the whistling duck   hunted for her eggs
   knotted grasp of grenadia vines   thin-skin hibiscus
   that gives and gives
                    scattering pollen like stars

in this garden the white man veils his face
from his gods   shears the land for it to look like him

in the leaves' tender shadow   he poisons the soil
with his spilling anger   his barbed sorrow

mout, muh body spread out, squeezin di coast like a jamette. Yes I's a jamette, and muh chin up high.

smell of a burning in the distance
whispers of uprisings in faraway fields

here   in the breath before
the blisters of night's long work
I listen to an old woman's
stories of yesterday:

the cacique   named for
the golden flower   whose words
danced on the kingfisher's feathers
her areytos echoing beyond her body
stirring every breeze

the one-armed maroon who
sowed   freedom's seed
wielding roots   and leaves   like warriors
slipping their toxic juices   into
the mouths of the masters

Drink and be cunt-drunk. Drink and drown, sinkin down in muh bone yard. But yuh have to come

until I can eat   what my hands
have made   I am a castaway   a hound's
hound tied up   skin gnawed down   gleam
of bone in the arrowed sun

                    what kind of life
we do and do   till clear dig   grind
months   years   measured by cane

                                    melody of home: a ruthless drift
                                    a song   that doesn't return

.

correct when it come to me. Yuh have to touch me, praise me, treat me like a queen. So bring di duck, di

I dreamed the sea scabbed over   a hush
across her black-blue lips   the scaled mother
below   circling   swimming the wound   the scaled
mother   hurling her body
        against the crust of hurt

pickaxe of tail and spine   until there   an opening:

O my forgetful, singed love
our sea is not   can never be the wound

                    we   shadows beneath shadows   stone interred
                    in stone   I   somebody I daughter
                    of seagrass   I don't always remember when
                    the hoe flings its dirt   against the coming dark

white roses, white wine and honey. Sweeten up muh pum pum. Make muh belly feel good. I here doin

words I can't speak   cause I don't want
my flesh to remember   but the stink
collects there   mapping
a route to my head

I want memory to fail   I want
to drive it out with the scent of pésil
to crush its mocking skull
pound it like garlic in a pilon

no memento but myself   no bead
from my grandmother's hair   my father's
singing calabash

just this hardened flesh
                              shard of the origin

me. Flowin how I does always flow but everybody does do what dey want wit me. Say dat I's yemaya

I won't leave
no memento of me
if the great god grants me
one thing

no sons or daughters
to stock the mills
no sons or daughters
pockmarked with price

and mizuchi, and how venus shell out sheself from me. Say in muh body is all kind ah king and beast.

bark of weeping dragon blood tree
leaves of asosi and rue   bitter tea
made to expel   I pour myself

red river floods the valley

I drain the weight
                    the sale of my womb

praise the blood   the vomit in the cane
the flies hoisting a kingdom there

bless the hummingbird   her fugitive wings

how she sucks and spreads
                    the medicine across the lip of the hill

Even Miss Ting, Miss Poet who tink she writin me here, gimme dis voice like a voice dat she fraid to

O horizon and deep sky   hex me to be sexless like the mermaid
hunkered into her scales   a shut sweetness I am not offered
the cool privacy of fish   I see no use for all these doors if they
do not serve me first   I envy the stone   the ordinary shoe   somehow I
more object than they   knowing line in the sky   salt and dry me   fuse me
out of use

forget. Syntax cut up and wring up wit chado beni and congo poppor. So I go take di voice and make it

15

rituals of numbing
tafia peeling the skin of my throat
bath of floating white petals

tafia cuts a lover
from the night's black silk

blade of hipbone
gulf river well sea

the dark's gourd   pouring the sky
across the peaks of my body

sing. Make it roar like I hittin di peak ah muh pleasure. But oh god dat chile does worry. Dat poet does

woman   woman   word hoarded
for madame   brooding in her paradise
her house-bound skin

how she flaunts her womanness   in lace
in the glow of her god   her god the rare thing
she has made   how she flaunts her talents
of fanning flies hiding from mosquitos raiding
the mansion

woman washed and patted dry with cotton
frail as a paper doll   woman
who watches us   with maliced eye
as if we   have stolen her cargo held a torch
to her ships

us dung-flung

pushed
                    to the edges of woman

turn and turn she mind wuss dan a wave. Hear what happen. I was at di center ah dis book, ah what

I am no hero   not bold or blessed
with the word's fluid music
like the warrior   shipped here
from another island
fusing gods and faiths to split chains

no secret listener of the whites' two-tongue
talks of liberty   equality   fraternity

no manbo at bwa kayiman
vessel for the twin-scarred spirit
pooling the might of the heavens
knifing the throat of the black pig

she call it? Di narrative. But she, Miss Poet push me out! Okay, lemme talk truth. Not all di way out but

water   the first language

I chant to the water
to flood my veins with
the voices of those who
were here before

when my sea-spirit rises
out of the waves and spins
a wreath onto my head
who then
is my master   what
claim of brand
upon my flesh

when my sea-spirit enters
I am cast from my body's tethers
I am no slave
I am the first language
spinning spinning
beyond the fields

down down to di bottom, somewhere she call di margins. I used to be on every kiss-muh-ass page,

does the goddess make me
        or I   the goddess

if she drags   me under
will my neck swell with the gift of gills   will I
touch my once-held home my land and its stolen light

O dust song blown through my grandmother's lips
   boy I watched with the flame tree's petals

        will I return to the place
rooted on memory's broken coast
that place   that girl who bathed
in the scent   of sun-dried raffia

if I make the goddess
if she drags me under
if my hair whitens washed in her salt
if the drowned bones meet me in the current's cool altar
if bone if coral if cowrie if I

muh waves rearin up tall, rollin tru lines and stanzas, bangin up white space. Yuh shoulda see muh

my hands my womb   whittled to a tool
        to build what   a white man's skulled temple
        his leaning empire of ash and bone

his coffee his cane arrows towards the death
of everything   the land chewed up
the skinned forests   his god within the vulture's jaw
the island made into a wicked stain a lump
in the throat of my mother

but if not here then where   crude shadow of home
my blood my grief glistens the soil
the land and me stubborn kin   the land made me
a new being forged of a greedy flame

        my blood already here
        my gods breathing in the hills
        in the slow tilt of evening

my gods stir me into a battle song:
    my muck my cane my muddy island my life my death my cliffs my body's bloom

power, muh bam bam swingin! But lawd, di gyal start to overtink. She say she feel like I was fightin

I sea child   child of currents yielding my conch to the mill
haunt of sugar   cutting my meat like sand   the world
gorges in the lick   bits of me   sliced off into the grains

my unbroken toil
my churn distilled

let the ocean's worms scatter when they split
my belly   let the ocean's worms burrow
into their throats   O water hemlock   sprout
from the grave mouth of my shell
your poisoned roots seizing their eyes
and joints blistering the organs

let them twitch and convulse
in the unconquerable rage name
of my mother

she. Like I was draggin she deeper into muh hole – and I should let allyuh know muh hole nice like a

they will say miracle
when what they mean is thirst
tongue jettying   awaiting runaway fist of rain
miracle   when what they mean is war song learned by limb
before the capture   sweet mixing of herb before the
capture   soldiers   head knotted with coordinates
strategy of flame the haunt   the memory of how
the bird taunts the river with its wing
and a sweet free thrust in a moon-drunk room
juices seeping into mattress   into coconut fiber
fermenting

miracle of breath and blood   miracle of a haunting
freedom never forgets where it once roamed   stalks me
til I can't sleep for want of the sea
til poison floats like a fly in the tea

freedom: ruthless siren   hurl and shriek
louder   than a dream

good lick ah mango chutney but dais a story fuh a next day – so yes, she feel like I woulda drown she

my sea-spirit rises
gleaming upon the shore
sharpening me into a blade

spit of rum   fist of cowrie
    flit of bird wing carving the breeze

a measured spine   rivaling the trees
a nipple becoming a compass
    or an eye

trumpet and fish

touch of her scales incites the hills

O mama   O mermaid   O wild hair dripping black
brush your spine up against the night
till it rips like the cry of a trumpet   tonight you
thirst for flame   tonight your water
is a burning field tonight fire fire fire

and all ah dem pages. She say she have to take back control. She say she di captain, di boss woman, di

what smoke
what threadbare cry
what child strung between
what architect of light
what leaf for the wound
what mountain and scar
what keloid
what mother
what sweat in the eye
what sojourning soul
what thrust in the dark
what hole
what belly
what babe without breath
what route to the hills
what dance
what drumbeat to call
what freedom
what body
what precipice of hope
what danger
what master
what whalebone
what poisoned meat
what pillaged field
what noise against the cane
what blaze
what sky
what name to call myself

one with di pen. She say she cyah be here fuh how many years wrestlin, gettin fling up in di waves. She

I seize the sugar mill's singing throat
crush its hymn   its grind nailed
to a settler's lust   merciless thief
of land limbs

if I could
         unrip   untear   unshread
the fingers   forearms   fed whole
to its unforgiving gnash

we feed the palaces   cathedrals
skeletal   looming   casting
their shadows across the earth

our bodies shoved into the mouths of discovery
civilization's march towards more
and more   comforts
for the cult of the whitened god

say some ting bout di human bein at the center, yuh know, di one she dream up from history. Real

could I give back the cruelties   the torture to its owner
beast   of fleur de lis
hissed hot into my flesh   its petals curling
into horns   the brand's stubborn stench
staking my nostrils

ruthless americas   islands of industry
I give what is mine to give
I return the wound

baccanal I tellin yuh. But doh worry bout me. I good. It have enough strengt down in di bottom.

they scream into the night   that it's the end
of the world   they shout into the flames
that it's the end of the world

they'll thirst for the end
before the halt of my body's capital

each chained morning was the end of our world
each night haunted by winds of another people's
end of world

let them ring the torched bell
of their beloved doomsday

Power wukkin up, churnin in di margins. Down here I does feel it all. Every drop ah blood. Every piece

I bow not to the lust   the greed that
chained me to this rock   the throb and pulse
the rot   the cock climbing skyward
leaking like an eye   not to their ambition
harvest of breasts and teeth   their dream
to make me unreal   to make me a voiceless fog
not to the eyes that watch me
when I make love   to my gods
as if my hips wind   for their boundless gaze
their thrill and fear   as if they
the center of my worship
          I bow not to the warped
envy of my sorrow   my songs stained in ink
of indigo   my dark hands marred
my sweat of nectar's ilk   my strained muscle
my keloids   forming a new muscle

ah flesh and bone. Every fish scale glitterin in di moonlight. Every feather draggin tru di salt. I does feel

praise the first spirits of this soil   of cassava
and rain   one-eyed goddess of the hurricane
her swift arms of thunder   lightning flood

praise the spirits who journeyed across the seas
to guard against forgetting
of crossroads and honeyed rivers
of iron and rum   of serpents
and the rainbow's hissing light

praise the mountains who gave the island
her true name   who guards the rebels
the scarlet milkweeds   korosol
inkberry and tamarind

praise our mothers' fading homes
which we may only see in dreams

it. And all ah dem does become part ah me. And I keep dem, all dey sound and feelin, I does keep dem

praise my dark hands that thread needles
and brew tea and slither when the rada
drums call me to dance the yanvalou and
clean wounds and wield blades and draw
blood and burn bagasse and logwood
and cacao   charting the course for the flame
praise the flame   it's vengeful hunger
feasting on the cane

deep in muh body. Everybody mudda know dat when yuh hold di conch shell mout to yuh ear, yuh go

praise my womb and the herbs' offering
of choice the souls floating free
swimming the realms of possibility
unborn   unforced
unbroken by whip   unnamed
by coffee's currency

hear muh voice ringin tru yuh head. "The sea," people does say in a dreamy little voice. "The song of the

ocean   O ocean
I forgive you   for not sinking
the ship to a water-grave   stripping
it clean to bone   for not dragging
me down to your halls of coral
a hurt I kept in the fruit of my love
like a poisonous seed

sea-spirit goddess mermaid
shimmering star of saltwater
I praise you for breath
the gift of tomorrow

sea." And yes, dey know di song but what dey doh know is di notes. And dey doh know what make up

I begin again   I begin
in black smoke washing
the island   barreling across fields
into sea
            what of country   of nation
of child's palm in my palm then
leaping through small streams
                what do I know
but my body now   my body making
itself free   onward onward
toward a beginning   in one hand
my machete   in the other the sea horn
the conch blaring the notes of my song

di notes, like where di notes come from. Like when fish does sing songs in di mornin and evenin when

&

"She a piece ah watergrass. Anywhere I throw she, she could grow."
— Eutrice Lewis

Guesswork

True: there is no homeland. Just my veined feet wandering the shore, marring paradise. Regretful inconvenience I am, smudged in the eye of a tourist's camera. *Vagrant.* Is what I learned to call the man with snarl of sky for a roof. And how now that word turns inward, taking root within the spleen. I am not lost or am I. *Light a white candle,* says a friend, his pupils storming within mine. *Neighbor it to a glass of water.* Flame and water to uncover a path, to greet the ones who walked moons before. Damn near atheist on so many days, but I touch the flame to the wick and my head is light light, it's lifting. Diasporan daughter, raking the soil for a map, a glint of my mama's gold, a bone to call my own.

See me: Saga gyal in kente pum pum shorts, thighs shea buttered, fulani hoops twisting a secret beside my face. I fix my mouth to say black girl. I twist my tongue to say magic. Yet when the day turns, I scorn this empty-bellied scavenging, the traditions fumbled then swirled to mud.

I want to say I am from nowhere and everywhere. But that feels coy like I am lifting my skirt for the empire's gaze. Even if it is true. On my papers and certificates, there is a country and another country. I can reach beyond, trace the soils through a strand of hair or swab of cheek. But what after? Forever of lineage riven and ruptured. So I search only because I can and sometimes I exist more and more each day, a brown cotton doll stuffed and stitching the X
for her own inadequate eye.

dey swimmin tru di coral? Well some ah di notes come from dat. And when dem children kickin up

Ma and the Snake

It must've been the third trimester
when my mother put down seeds at the side of the house
still under construction. She had always heard a pregnant woman's
hand could spring forth the richest crop, and though skeptical
she planted pigeon peas, bird peppers, broad-leaf thyme
and they came in thick and fragrant, nourished by my waxing
heart and sea-blast.

On an ordinary day, in the carnival season's dry heat
while picking the sweet bellies of pigeon peas, a horsewhip
slid among the leaves, proclaimed its black mouth and split tongue.
Everyone warned that my speech would be marked, nicked
by the snake's jealous hiss. My mother swept their forecasts
to the road, thought it nothing but old island talk,
kin to the cow-foot woman and douen.

My no-nonsense mother, mother of the rosary's
swift reason, still believes my tongue was fluent
as tadpoles in the creek. How eager she is to forget
that in my earliest years, the horsewhip's lisp rose from my lips
and my cousins begged me to spit out words like *season* and
souse, charmed by the pink head
peering out between my teeth. I was a child of thorn
and shadow, drawn to the soil's mysteries, peculiar as
the driftwood's rot. What dark-throated truths
piped into my mouth, what stinging languages
broken and blown, fed to my gorging breath.

foam and laughin when dey fly dey kite on di beach? Right, well some ah it come from dat. But some

First American Years

Me and my brother stare at the skies, waiting for snow. Just 50 degrees, but we don't yet know the cold. Before this, a sun scorching the asphalt well before noon. Rainflies flooding the porch, dragging in their warm, wet season.

Our father in the flesh. No longer over the phone, or in cards or letters stamped with the American flag.

The new school wants to know if I can read *cat, dog, hat.* I think they think big words don't exist on islands.

A music video for Biggie. Faith's candle-lit croon hemming the shroud of the weeping city.

Ma studies to assure America that she can do what she's done for years. Before this, she listened closely to hearts in utero. Guided the newcomers through canals.

Visits to my aunt in East New York, who laughs like the riddim section at a cricket match. Her neighbor below banging on the ceiling with a broom.

Abner Louima survives the police. The horrors of his assault on loop. Three major surgeries to mend his body.

A hall of fossils is my father's church. Saint Triceratops, its trinity of horns. Saint Stegosaurus, of the pilgrimage spine. He teaches us his creeds: the holy biomes, the artifacts almighty.

On the news, a painting of the Black Virgin Mary. The mayor's rage sets him ablaze. Tirades against oil, elephant dung, collage and glitter.

ah it come from dem men fightin fuh gold and diamond and oil. And land. Everybody want land,

I learn to turn double dutch without clipsin. Collect Spice Girls stickers. Read *too many ah dem babysitter's club books.* Sing *do you eat ba-con do you eat ba-con yes baaay-beh* on the school playground. Sing *scrubs* and cruising *drop tops.* Trade my dreadlocked soca crushes for boy bands.

On a field trip to a museum, a white boy I don't know tells me he's glad Martin Luther King, Jr., is dead.

Amadou, O Amadou. Like all Black innocence: chopped down, stolen, gone too soon.

The winter winds eat through me, through my first puffy jacket, the bulky long johns. The cold cracks my lips though Ma coats them thick with vaseline.

murderin wit dey god name in dey mout. Blood bubblin up from crabhole. Blood stainin di shore. And

La Divina Pastora, Mother of Miracles

We cast down our burdens at the feet of the *Black Mother* us of myriad stripes   hindu
and catholic   junctioned by her body   here in the southwest of Trinidad.

La Divina Pastora

of disputed origin like all women blessed   or caught in the latitudes
        of conquest and myth.

Once a girl who grew to a woman   *Patron Saint of Siparia* before nightfall. Once a statue
sprung from soil of cacao.   gowned in white and gold
bestowing us with sight   or husbands or whatever
we ask. We ask   day in and out   sweaty pilgrims with our hard
won knots   our battered backs   our   tears and
haberdashery.

Madonna Murti

speaks to me   through her burglar proof
glass and in the creep of memory   I lock the bedroom door against the
handyman's routine gaze. I shield my   pubescent body.   She too

plenty notes come from dem ship flyin dey sail and country flag high high like cobo wing. Longtime,

Mother of Miracles

coin offerings pocketed   rosary
dress hem sullied by the traffic of hands.
against the muck   the world's leaking
her and she lets us cry out her many

with her own memories:
snatched   crown rushed to pawn shop
She too trapped in her protection   caged
desires. We ask and she gives. We wrong
names.

Divine Shepherdess
Supari Mai
Black Virgin

and blooms of tulsi. We gather in procession
Friday. We bring our children to shear their first hairs.
jewelry flowers olive oil. We fill her cup
to her worth   but by what measure?

who once roamed banana leaves
down Coora Road on Good
We litter the altar with rice
to lip   think its flood climbs close
Whose thirst?

dey used to shoot cannon by di ton, coughin up gunpowder over di water. Nowadays is bomb and

Extra Virgin Olive Oil

after Walter Price's painting

Look once: and it's her fingers that pull you in
the absence of them, how they've disappeared
within her, splitting her body like reeds
at the river's lips. Bantu Knotted American
Queen, pedestaled at the top of the canvas.
Spill of red paint, blue drip of stars
pooling the foot of the nation.

Look again: not a clit
but a book that occupies the hand
and you smile at how easy it is
to mistake one pleasure for another
membrane for membrane
twin yearnings for the flesh-spit of knowledge
for after all, to know
is to let the sweet waters run
down down the slope
the purple mountains.

Stare until the painting becomes a mirror
until you are sixteen again in your room
with Jimi Hendrix plastered on the wall
like a saint. You are clutching a book
blotting the ink with your sweaty palms
shoving the words into your mouth
practicing, repeating, drilling an American accent
sloughing the saltwater off your tongue
speaking yourself into disappearance.

bullet. Yuh ever hear bout Carib's Leap? Down in Grenada? Or I should say Camerhogne cause dais

And you would have disappeared
were it not for the pussy's pages
how turning them lit the tunnel into
yourself, to the books that could only be read
in salt and seaweed, and the touch that made you
crave your own dark scent. What tiny stars you
are, spilling.

what di Kalinago name di place. Dem Kalinago resist dem settlers full force, but arrow wasn't no match

Woman in Dub

after Lee "Scratch" Perry and Max Romeo's song "Chase the Devil"

Side A.

The devil I see is the one I saw   and nail out of fears   out of cycles of wound
dread calcifying into prophecy   I put on an iron shirt to face it chase it but the cop
still piss drunk with power I put on an iron shirt but the men on the street surveil
the nipple   been hounding my punani since   before I spilled my first blood
what a menace of a body   I hurl blame to the husk   is the devil real or is it of my
fantastical making   the answer is not the matter   the fact of paranoia be the true
violence   warfare: the very presence of the question   I want to peer inward   to
take a good look at the soundsystem   my heartbeat echoing out of my folkloric
thirst   my desperate belief in other realities   a B-side where I'm abolished from
emotional labor aka black woman's burden   free to surrender to my own madness
to sink down into the dub of it   stripped of my first voice   reverbing outside the
pain of a body —

fuh cannon and gun. Di ones who survive couldn't bear to surrender so dey leap off a cliff to dey death

44

Side B.

        stripped of my first voice

               down in the dub   cop hounds my blood

into paranoia   a black reality

                  cycles spilled

       power husked

                          emotional woman I   I

I iron   real street   folkloric and mad

                       tr tr trrrruuuueeee

take a good look at the devil

               peer into the dread

men surrender to wound: drunk   calcified   but I

       fantastic

                 chasing echoes

 nailed to system   free in sound

          I   a fact

               answer of my own making

in the sea. I does still feel di ripples tru-out muh body. And I still feelin di ripples ah di Middle Passage.

Fleshed Cartographies:

after Katherine McKittrick

a blood work, akin to the moon's map, its shadowed witness, its rerouting through a house of skin, pulped and spilling down the thigh; small breath into soil choked with haints. To explore the escape: body lilting across the uncharted edge of terrain; or the unescape: fallopian as factory assembling tools to tend the field, lubrication as evidence of a weeping or a wound. The exploration: not a dwelling in but the carving of a desire line, a new footpath to the oracle's ear, reseeing the past to replot the prophecy.

And I feel all di people who squeezin deyself onto dem brukup little boat, riskin everyting cause

Harriet Jacobs Grips the Silence

Disappear me

in the 5x7x7 hull

        of the blue-strangled attic.
        Mice brush against
        this thigh like the beard
        of a man who owns nothing
        but the light and my toothless
        dreams where I crack
        an egg like night and pour
        into my daughter's dead hair

me   a crack of air

squatting the unseen rows between the panels

whispering through

    the cherry tree's hacked offering.

Mice brush like money

      toes
      neck

      the secret autobiographies
      stolen away to the fingernail's cave.

Me, a spectered footstep
plunged from the ear
dissipating into the black room

heedful as needle embroidering silk.

Through the window: sky pushed back
a stained sheet of wind.

Acres of tobacco, limbs
skin rusting on the line.

somebody greed mash up dey country, and when dey finally see di shore of anodda country, di

Malady

How does it enter? Through nostril? Or through the mouth, dissolving on the tongue then sliding down the throat? Maybe it wedges itself beneath the toenail, finding a roof there, a shelter for a season's rest. There's talk about the one that enters when somebody cuts you deep, the one that tunnels your heart, inches up up and blows out all the candles in the room. They say that one sucks the guts and marrow till you're a net of bones, nearly scattering at the edge of a bed. But no one knows if it's like that, really. And no one knows how it enters, or when. Does it come at the moment of the inhale before the first cough? Or in time with the first pinch of the aching knee? Is it years before that? Before you learn to thread a sewing machine? To cook beneath the sky in a coal pot, throwing coconut shells into the fire; when pain was predictable and understood, when it had a clear cause: the prick of a needle, the lick of a flame?

upstandin citizens does push dem back in di sea. All ah dat, all ah dat hurt and grief and hope and

Dancing at the Shrine in Harlem

If not to mirror the span of the swan
pulling out of the swamp
scarring the water with its absence
the story unveiled in the movement of weeds
then salt
      then wet wood   then muse alight

then I touch his wrists and the way he moves then this
is the goddess choosing this roof and drop of rain

and I forget about the rumor of my limbs
how they once roamed the horizon like wolves

      If not the swan
          then who   then I've hemmed myself
          into a purple light

If the drum has slipped into my lungs

If he is no longer man but the breath of a humming candle

If he is not man but a broad leaf praising the voyage of the rain

If salt could dissolve into the low haunt of bass
          then I am and I am

rage. All dat stolen life, dat raw weepin deep into me. Dat is di notes ah muh song. Dat is what yuh

It's Risky to Love in the Season of Hunters

I.

And when the dark tightens
around my neck I think
of vultures casting a shadow
before the flesh breaks

of the omen of crows
nailed into the sky
of gaping earth-home
for a Black child

fear my sisters, my lover
will cross a hunter's eye
and writhe into horned creatures
to be gunned down
or strung up

that they walk with the promise
of carrion splayed
for the flies.

And when the dark trickles
down my throat I know
that home is but a fading horizon
that here, I will always be
out of body, I will always fall

outside the lines, that if I dare
go missing, my name
will crawl beyond
the reach of memory

that I am only a problem, a pest
a damned spot, a gamebird
a bullseye, a neck
for a hook
a haunted, hunted thing.

hearin when yuh hear muh voice tru di conch shell mout. All dat sound and feelin. It have to come out

II.

When I heard the news of the trial, that there'd be no justice for Trayvon, my
body collapsed into itself. Becky picked my lungs up off the floor. Said I would
need them for dancing. What I needed was to be home in my neighborhood of
foreigners with our chimera accents. I needed the coffin silence of the Q85 bus
cruising down Merrick Blvd, the secret mourning of women behind the frayed
curtains of their weaves, the churn of the engine emitting all our trapped sounds.

III.

These friends
who smile
cry   twerk
praise Wu Tang
snap fingers
ask if our hair
is real
study
walk arm
in arm
talk
like family
break bread
share cropped t-shirts
ice cream
at the mall
at the river
with us? Who
are they really
if they do not
lament our dead?

somehow. But I doh only sing from shell. When di wave stand up angry like a big, strapid giant. When

Island

Someone brought the map from another country, walking with a back cutlass straight, pointing skyward from soil. Someone wrapped it in cotton t-shirts, laid it down as one would a homebound grandmother, laid it down in a suitcase.

Someone hung it on the wall, on the eyeball of a nail, in the too small living room or in the kitchen where it would brace against steam.

Beautiful map, made of thin black velvet. Outlined in sequins, or silver dust or blue ink. Haboring ghosts in the threads.

Inside its border is the image of a hummingbird angled above a red hibiscus. Or an aging monument left by gold-seeking explorers. And squeezed in between the images are the names of places:

Siparia. Icacos
inching down the coast
towards Serpent's Mouth.

Outside the map, outside the border, are no hummingbirds or silver dust. There are mugs with dried cocoa cracking on the rim. There are bills snarling out the mouths of their envelopes. There are smudges and breadcrumbs and names slapped on prescription bottles. There is snow, ice, leafless trees.

Mum map. Silent map.
Map won't say "Daughter, daughter,
bring your wrecked body home."

di hurricane twist and roar out ah me. People like to say is god or is devil, but dat force, dat wild energy

A Retrograde

She crept into my room, took me outside into the mosquito night thick with the gutted hums of fishermen's wives, piercing the flesh of a sleep walking sky.

She taught me that cobwebs are hammocks for spirits, a stop along the way to rest their weary skins, a knot on the thread of their pilgrimage to a place they had almost touched once.

In those days, a village could grow legs. Wedge itself deep into the throat of mountains where horses couldn't smell it, where footsteps couldn't sear its memory onto peeling roads.

Dear mama: The orchids have teeth.
The machetes are ornaments
 rusting upon the walls.

I want to build you a temple
of teeth
but my hands are too tender,
my hands are for stringing
he rice grains of rosaries.

Dear mama: On the ocean roams a shadow of splinters.
The fish are hurling themselves onto the shore.
The shore will break into birds of dust.
The scales are mirrors
 blinding the sun.

On the ocean roams a shadow of splinters.
How will I swim to you
when the day is done?

is really just people, is really all livin tings. All dey sound and feelin spillin out from muh belly. But ont

Orfeu Negro / Black Orpheus

after Marcel Camus' 1959 film

poor blacks   sweet blacks   molasses-smeared and sticky blacks
blacks in favela erect   hoisted high in scorched hills   blacks in blue
in white in yellow dresses   blacks yielding kites to the wind   serene
blacks   toothless blacks   beige brown black blacks   blacks nested
in hammocks being tropical blacks   blacks hawking squid and onions
hustlin blacks   cans of oil on their heads blacks   blacks summoning
sun from sea   slit-throat rooster blacks   blacks hazed in lust in lazy heat
dust blacks   spiced blacks   watermelon blacks   water dog sailor blacks
blacks whirling gold thread for carnaval   starfall blacks   star-crossed blacks
blacks busting through bas relief bossa nova blacks   glistening blacks
masked blacks   blacks in pretty painted shacks   crucifix blacks
nightfall blacks   shadow blacks   tristeza the sadness
so sweet it rots black

I tell yuh bout Miss Ting? Miss Poet? Bout how di human at di center? Is funny. Big Me, wit all dis

I too from masquerade land. Asphalt sputtering, chomping on plastic beads and feathers, costumes re-singing histories of the flesh. My island a speck, a globe of spit slipping past the eye of the world. So I watch *Orfeu Negro* greedy for a glimpse of myself, a skip trick of light splayed out on the screen. My greed, my open mouth cares not for taste. I am almost ashamed. I want to be looked upon as the world looks upon Eurydice. Delicate, the way her pistil sways in the breeze.

O thirst of commerce, ever-sucking despite force of flow, pitching our flesh from port to port. Aren't we charmed and exquisite, dancing as we've always danced, drenched in our cane-taint?

power, all dis goodlookin flesh dat yuh body cyah ignore. I have to squeeze up muhself inside she idea. I

Swig of dawn, orchid's exhale
hounds the cliff. Camera's invitation: see

the bodies framed by fronds of paradise. No space
for my mourning. The dirge is drowned in the bay.

Children twist limbs
to dance, hoisting the sun
with guitar strings.

No space for my —

Orfeu gone. Eurydice dissolved
in the plucked refrain.
Where a black falls, another

dances up from the soil. Happy blacks, cycle
of blacks, kicking up dust.

have to look where she lookin. Talk how she want me to talk. I have to make muhself a woman. Make

Accent

Don't ask me why I say \ wor-tuh \
in one sentence, then
\ war-der \ in the next. You already
know. It's not difficult
to understand. It's that you choose
not to. The jury is still out
on whether being from just
one country is a luxury
or a limitation
but you should know
why, how
a voice, an accent
drifts between the sounds
of two or more shores.

All your first world knowledge
and you still can't help
but say what you do
or don't detect
as if I am trivia
as if my voice
is contraband
smuggled
through your God-
given borders.

muhself a goddess. Make muhself whatever she need me to be. And she need me to be plenty. She need

Ex(ile)

We ask about our people and they tell us the plight of boats
yachts smashed in the marina, ferries crashed into harbors
masts snapped, propellers bent, vessels drowned in coves.

They broadcast reports of water rising in hotel rooms
sand slipping into sheets where our cousins could never sleep
salt stains as testimony, spit-prints of the hurricane's wrath.

Bodies are piling up in the morgues and instead
an elegy of boats
an inventory of industry, countdown
to when paradise can begin again.

So it seems when we're no longer property
we become less than property
a nail sick with rust, jangling in high winds.

This would be a different story were it not
for ex(ile), whose sting swells when banished
in one's own yard, barred
from the fruits of your mother's land.

Inside ex(ile): tempests and fault lines
are developers' wet dreams.
A mainland will sink its territory in debt
starve its subjects in the wake of storms
clearing ground for palaces on the shore.

Inside ex(ile): the body is only
as good as its technology
how it buckles in a field.

Inside ex(ile) is the ile
pushed across the Atlantic through Oya's lips.
Place or shelter, sacred home.

me to be a keeper ah all she memory. She need me to be di time before she move to a strange new

We ask about our people and fill the silence with prayer
utterances rerouting to our climate's first spirits:
Guabancex blowing furious winds, Huraca'n spiraling at the center.
Guatauba drenched in thunder and lightning.
Coatrisque of the deadly floods.

Spare our kin, we plead. Save your wrath for the profiteers.
Cast them from our archipelago, our ile ife of the seas
until home is a place we never have to leave.

country, before she feel di deep sadness creepin up like a man scalin a coconut tree. She need me to

Flowers Pressed to My Head

The mirror is not a home. Not the roof-slant of sunlight. Or a soft whistling sitting on the hill of morning. A windowpane, a storefront window wiped clean: Not home. I try to find myself there, in the light. There is nothing. But phantoms crooning, mouths wide, terrifying as lakes.

The mirror is not home without you. You hung the flowers, drying away from the light. The table, its leaning leg, its eggshell blue. You brought the bread. You wrote the dates on the underside of black and white photographs. Laid down dust on the books. Without you: bare wood and nails.

make she feel safe. Like I does do when di tumors in she womb makin she bleed heavy heavy fuh weeks,

I stood, stacked before the door like bricks. Stripped of gold and scent and sewn-in hair. Brittle, thirsting. Who will call to me, nested like this? Bare and unadorned is not me. Is not me.

All that stuff: plumes for the ego. I heard myself say it while stacked at the door. And the voice couldn't have come from the dying paint. Nor the wood nor the woman, pinned to the wall. I remember a man with hair hanging long; unknowable vines. I heard him say there is no me. There is I and I, which is you too. You and I intertwined. Snaked, rubbing skins. I'd like to stitch myself to the divine. To stitch myself, there must be no me. I must cover the me to make room. I must dig and bury the me. Which is to say I am floating on the light.

bleedin tru she clothes on di train. She does wonder how anybody does carry on wukkin and bonin and

Deep breaths to cough up the rust. To bleach out the sully. Morning finds me so, in a rush to clear a room for you. Deep breaths to cough up the rust, clumps of hair shoved in by the mothers and their mothers. Fathers, way across the sea even when they are planted on the front porch. I wish I had a front porch, a home for the rocking chair but I am scrambling for borrowed pieces of land, boxes with a few holes punched in. How deep the wound. So many tiles crowding the sky. How can I see my divine? If I can't see her then I'll make her see me. I will snip and stitch the strands. Round and round onto a stocking cap. I will string beads in the singing light. Sever the strands into the destined shape. End to end, a rope to the base of the sky. End to end, a family line.

makin pretty tings wit all di doubt and di pain dey totin. And sometimes I feel di same way bout me. At

This mound of strands is an invitation. I am bride and devotee. I am a horse. I have moved through the training. I will not go mad. I am vessel. I can dance the hollow beneath the skin. I can pour the rum for you to drink. I line my forehead with your favorite flowers. I will dance the broken toed dance. I will leap in the likeness of your flight. Bring me to the brush and I'll tap out this rhythm. Carve out a space with a comb. Dig, dig. Or climb. Up and down is the same.

my big ole age, I still cyah deal wit everything dat I feel. Is like di past always wit me. Always cyclin tru.

The head is the seat of the spirit. The head is where the spirit enters. Where the spirit is housed. The head needs a covering beyond what we were born with. Some wear hats. Like those women in church who clasp hands and fan the air. The women who will catch you. Who will hold up your body when the spirit weakens your knees. Some wear scarves. Or wraps. I wear strands and strands sewn by worn hands. I wear a crown of hair. A throne for the spirit. When I walk they fall to their knees. When I walk they turn heads and kiss lips and call out praises. I, divine. One with the pavement or gliding on tar.

Dais why I keep so many rituals, so many habits ah bein. I try to keep muh movements regular, keepin

Goddamn I'm pressed against the light. Bone-white. Or is it bone-straight? What color is the divine? My head is heavy. I cannot hold up my head. Where are the ladies? The women dressed in white? Hold me up, against.

time like a real riddim specialist. Most ah di time I does get it right. And everybody does be happy

Wind-blown. Bone-straight. Bone-white as the breathless. Strung bone up to make music out of wind. Whisper of the divine at the meat of my scalp. Touch me like I am a vessel. Like I am the horse. In the morning. In the river mist of oil sheen. In my chest, a village. Fill me I am hungry. I am stained to the pavement. The measured strands, silver in the light.

when muh tides and currents keep di beat. When I give and give and give. And I doh mind givin,

Chant for the Waters and Dirt and Blade (Slight Return)

Brooklyn, NY 2019

a memory of the cemetery flooded
with the murmur of the living   the candles' small fires
nesting on the graves   my grandfather and we his thin-limbed
offspring every year in the humid dark each all saint's day
the mosquitos rising from the grasses to feed
every year we light   we pray that our dead
will not forget the chant below our skins

the scent of melting wax will always
call forth the memory of our dead   the unheard footfalls
the bodiless rustling through the dasheen leaves

whedda is fish or islands or medicine, if is salt fuh sore and wound. But di trouble is when I doh get

on this hallow's eve I am listening
to the cars sounding their grievances on flatbush avenue
while hemming words in my apartment   wishing that I
could wake up tomorrow   in my first country
to visit what remains of my grandfather
to go to him   to the cemetery of his mother
his father   and the wax riding the damp air
its fragrance winding beyond
the dark palm prints of a bois canot tree

anyting back. Or when what I gettin back is oil spill. Is sewage. Is all kind ah plastic. Dem kind ah ting

who   what   how do I believe? my worship colonized
my gods painted in a foreign face   my grief-song milked
in the razed woods   shipped off   most wanted
commodity
                                    I stuff my ears
against the old spirits' call fearful of the way the past
speaks to me   I cling to cold reason but find
empire's grasp especially there   I believe
in what makes me free   I believe in the red-hot
flowers crowning the head
of the flamboyant tree   I believe in nutmeg
ground down for cassava pone and the hands
the firm singing hands that push
its measurements   though the decades

does upset muh riddim. Does make me start to overheat. And when ting eh good fuh me, it eh good my goddess is

the wave unsheathing   my name
strung through

    the conch's contralto

fuh nobody. But dis is stale news. Everybody know happy bird does shit in dey own nest. And how

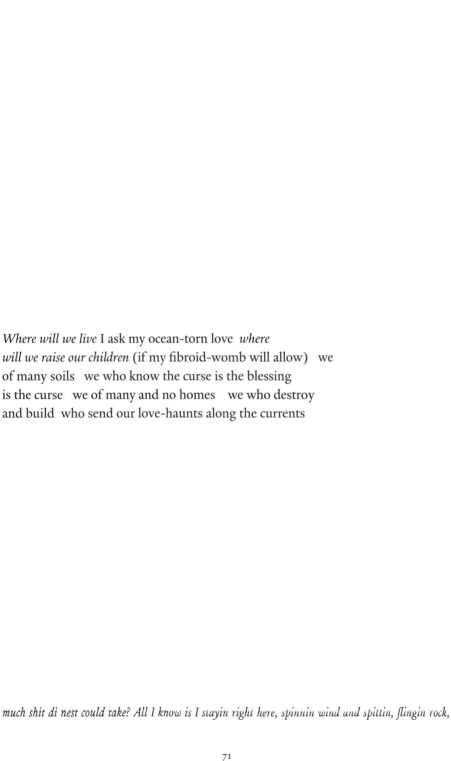

Where will we live I ask my ocean-torn love *where*
will we raise our children (if my fibroid-womb will allow)   we
of many soils   we who know the curse is the blessing
is the curse   we of many and no homes   we who destroy
and build who send our love-haunts along the currents

much shit di nest could take? All I know is I stayin right here, spinnin wind and spittin, flingin rock,

whether quick clapping of hands   or hymns of lambs
and mercy   or fistful of cowrie   thrown across a mat
or psalms to tread the lion   and the cobra   or symbols
drawn in cornmeal   guarded throughout the brutal passage

shell and seaweed against di coast, spreadin high and wide, survivin however I survive. And who cyah

I fear that I will never be fully at home
that the very first leaving cracked the skull
of my belonging   that when I eventually stop
moving I won't understand
the land's grieved tongue   I brown the sugar
in the heavy-bottomed pot   to fill up
every space   to remind myself of language

take di heat, well, yuh already know. I eh really come here to do all dıs talkın. I come to roll muh waves

I belong to the foam that singes
the sand where I was thrown to the waves
just weeks into the world   my eyes widening
to limestone cliffs   to sea almonds ripening
upon the shore   my hands are the scarlet ibises
soaring the salt-washed dawn
cleaving the sky open like a blade

and wine muh pretty body and roar till I black like basalt and roar till I black like basalt and sing.

Notes

Chant for the Waters and Dirt and Blade

The poem is set during the Haitian Revolution, in which Africans enslaved in the French colony of Saint Domingue fought for and achieved liberation. The colony was considered the most lucrative and one of the most brutal in the Americas. The revolution resulted in the creation of the first Black republic. Although the revolution was a success, France demanded reparations from the new nation of Haiti for each liberated person, whom it considered to be lost property. Haiti paid the modern equivalent of $21 billion to France.

The poem references Taíno cacique Anacaona, Maroon leader and Houngan François Makandal, early revolution leader, Muslim cleric, and Houngan Dutty Boukman, and Manbo and leader Cécile Fatiman.

The poem draws heavily upon the figure of Mami Wata, a water spirit revered throughout various regions of Africa and the African diaspora, often described as a mermaid. The poem also draws upon the figure of Lasirèn, an ocean lwa of Haitian Vodou, described as a mermaid, and who, according to some stories, has origins in the Congo and swam to Haiti alongside the ships of the transatlantic slave trade.

Epigraph by Eutrice Lewis

Eutrice Lewis was a health-care worker from Trinidad and Tobago who worked in New York for almost thirty years before returning to Fyzabad, Trinidad. She was also my grandmother.

First American Years

This poem refers to the slain Brooklyn rapper The Notorious B.I.G., the music video "I'll Be Missing You" by Puff Daddy, Faith Evans and 112, the painting "The Holy Virgin Mary" by Chris Ofili, the British music group the Spice Girls, the *Baby-Sitter's Club* book series by Ann M. Martin, the song "No Scrubs" by TLC, and the song "Nice and Slow" by Usher. I do not know the origin of the bacon song that was sung on the playground.

The poem also speaks of Abner Louima, a Haitian immigrant who was beaten and sexually assaulted by a New York Police Department officer with a broken broomstick while handcuffed at a Brooklyn precinct.

The poem also mentions Amadou Diallo, a twenty-three-year-old Guinean immigrant who was shot and killed by four New York Police Department officers in the doorway of his Bronx apartment building. The officers fired forty-one bullets; nineteen bullets struck Diallo.

Extra Virgin Olive Oil

The poem was inspired by Walter Price's painting of the same name. It was written for a poetry-visual art collaboration with the Studio Museum in Harlem's *Fictions* exhibit.

Woman in Dub

This poem is written in a form that I created to honor and emulate the structure of early Jamaican dub music, not to be confused with dubstep. It draws inspiration from the song "Chase the Devil" by Max Romeo, which was also sung and produced by the pioneering dub producer Lee "Scratch" Perry.

Fleshed Cartographies

This poem was inspired by the book *Demonic Ground: Black Women and the Cartographies of Struggle* by Katherine McKittrick, professor of Black and Gender studies.

Harriet Jacobs Grips the Silence

This poem refers to Harriet Jacobs, who hid in a crawl space for seven years during her escape from enslavement in North Carolina.

It's Risky to Love in the Season of Hunters

This poem refers to Travyon Martin, a Black seventeen-year-old high school student who was shot and killed by a neighborhood watch coordinator in Florida.

Orfeu Negro/Black Orpheus

In this poem, I grapple with my reactions to the film *Orfeu Negro,* made by the French director Marcel Camus in 1959. Although I enjoy the film's spectacular colors, soundtrack, Black representation, and focus on Carnaval, I am conflicted by its simplistic, idyllic, and patronizing depiction of Afro-Brazilians.

Sea Voice

The text running along the bottom margins of the book is written in my best approximation of the spoken colloquial form of Trinidadian English, which the late poet Kamau Brathwaite would have called "nation language."

Acknowledgments

My gratitude to the editors of the following publications in which these poems have appeared, some in earlier versions:

Academy of American Poets / Poem-a-Day: "Woman in Dub"

American Short Fiction: "Sea Voice"

Best American Poetry 2015 and *Muzzle Magazine:* "A Retrograde"

Callaloo and *Winter Tangerine:* Excerpts from "Chant for the Waters and Dirt and Blade"

The Collagist: "Malady Unlocks the Door"

Learn then Burn 2: "It's Risky to Love in the Season of Hunters"

Redivider: "Flowers Pressed to My Head"

The Rumpus: "Dancing at the Shrine in Harlem"

Winter Tangerine: "Extra Virgin Olive Oil"

Best New Poets 2020: "Orfeu Negro/Black Orpheus"

Thank you to the following institutions that have provided growth and support: New York Foundation for the Arts, Poets & Writers, Poets House, Kimbilio Fiction, The Charlestown International Maroon Conference, Callaloo Creative Writing Workshop, The Norman Mailer Center, The Conversation, Brown University's Literary Arts MFA, NYU's Creative Writing MFA, Georgetown University, Princeton in Africa, Youth Communications, Saint Ann's School, and Tagore's.

Immense gratitude to all my teachers and mentors, especially R. Erica Doyle, Aracelis Girmay, Kate Schapira, Deborah Landau, Sharon Olds, Yusef Komunyakaa, B. Anthony Bogues, Mark McMorris, Jennifer Fink, Brian Evenson, Renee Gladman, Carole Maso, Simone White, Natalie Diaz, Ravi Howard, Meena Alexander, Nita Noveno, Marline Martin, Mahogany L. Browne, Jive Poetic and J. P. Howard.

All my heart to my dear friends and peers for their wisdom, love, and support, especially Charleen McClure, Ebony Johnson, Yassi Tamdji, E. G. Asher, Katherine Agard, Dominique Barron, Diane Exavier, Jayson P. Smith, Nabila Lovelace, Yanyi, Dalia Elhassan, A. H. Jerriod Avant, Jeremy Michael Clark, Angel Nafis, Airea D. Matthews, Safiya Sinclair, Arielle John, Daria-Ann Martineau, Nicole McClure, Jazzmen Lee-Johnson, Rico Frederick, Ethel Amponsah, Shaniqua Martin, Michaela Henley, Linda Kaoma, Terry Ayugi, Nedjra Manning, Arvolyn Hill, Emily Crain-Lopez, Elias E. Lopez, Esmé M. Watkins, Nate Marshall, Alexandra Gauss, Alec Niedenthal, Kit Schluter, Jon Sands, Ricardo Maldonado, Timothy Edwaujonte, Ama Codjoe, Ashlyn Mooney, Shamara Wyllie Alhassan, Hadiya Sewer, Anna Thomas, and Bedour Alagraa.

All my love to my awe-inspiring ancestors, and to my beautiful family, especially Gloria Lewis-Bailey, Desmond Bailey, Althea Lewis, Ian Bailey, Monique Ransom, Bryan Brown, Nyron Bailey, Rhonda Bailey, Desmond Bailey, Jr., Keisha Oreesingh, Crystal Lewis, Walter Noel, Petra Schereka, Benjamin Schereka, Andrea Cozier-Ruiz, and their immediate families.

A special thanks to my NYU Poetry MFA and Brown Literary Arts MFA cohorts for your generosity. Thank you Ashley L. Cohen for inviting me to speak to your Revolution Literature class at Georgetown, and to Maxine Montilus, Riva Précil, and Cumbe Dance Center for the rich worlds of Haitian folkloric dance and other Afro-Caribbean dance.

Thank you Andrea Chung for your powerful art, and for providing the powerful "vex" face for this book.

Thank you Carl Phillips for your belief in this book, and thank you to the Yale University Press team.

Thank you Rebecca Nagel for your wisdom, advocacy and persistence.

And my deepest love and appreciation to my geliefste Wilton Schereka for your unwavering belief in me, for reading my poem drafts though you claim to be unqualified as a poet, for holding it down while I was on the mend and finishing this book, for your bold, imaginative, joyous love. Ek is lief vir jou.